The Entertainment Songbook

100 GREAT SONGS From HOLLYWOOD, BROADWAY And TELEVISION

Project Manager: Sy Feldman
Cover Design: Joann Carrera

Contents

AQUARIUS

Words by
JAMES RADO and
GEROME RAGNI

Music by
GALT MacDERMOT

From "ARTHUR," an Orion Pictures Release through Warner Bros.

ARTHUR'S THEME
(Best That You Can Do)

Words and Music by
BURT BACHARACH, CAROLE BAYER SAGER,
CHRISTOPHER CROSS and PETER ALLEN

Once in your life, you'll find ___
Ar - thur, he does what he

Arthur's Theme - 4 - 1

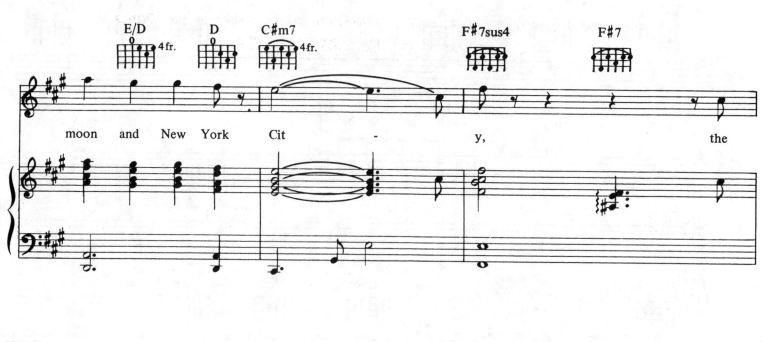

From the Soundtrack of PBS Series "THE CIVIL WAR," a Film by Ken Burns

ASHOKAN FAREWELL

By
JAY UNGAR

Ashokan Farewell - 3 - 1

12

From the Motion Picture "BATMAN" ™
THE BATMAN THEME

Music Composed by
DANNY ELFMAN

The Batman Theme - 5 - 1

BEAUTIFUL CITY

Words and Music by
STEPHEN SCHWARTZ

Beautiful City - 5 - 1

BEWITCHED

Words by
LORENZ HART

Music by
RICHARD RODGERS

Theme from *"UP CLOSE & PERSONAL"*

BECAUSE YOU LOVED ME

Words and Music by
DIANE WARREN

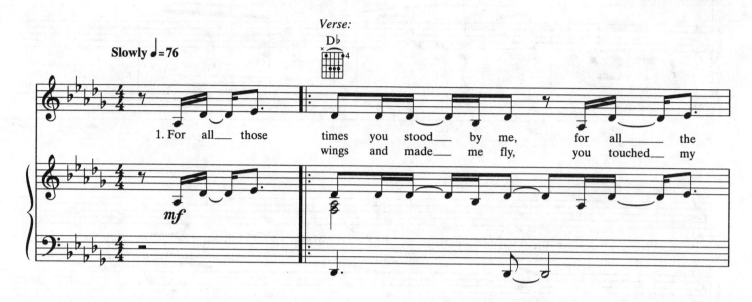

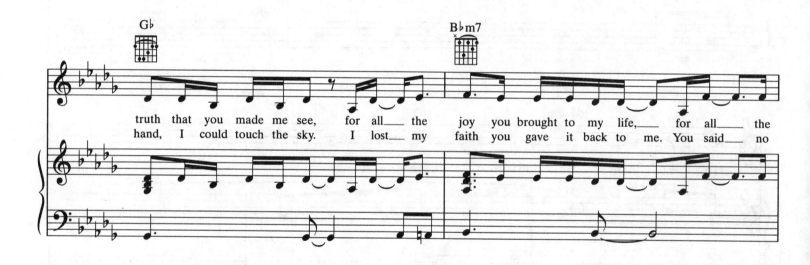

Because You Loved Me - 5 - 1

BIG SPENDER

Music by
CY COLEMAN

Lyrics by
DOROTHY FIELDS

Moderately, with a beat

The min-ute you walked in the joint, I could see you were a man of dis-tinc-tion, A

real Big Spend-er,___ good look-ing,___ so re-fined.___ Say,

would-n't you like to know what's go-ing on in my mind?_ So let me get right to the point,

Big Spender - 3 - 1

34

CABARET

Lyrics by
FRED EBB

Music by
JOHN KANDER

Cabaret - 3 - 1

Love Theme from "Superman"

CAN YOU READ MY MIND?

Words by
LESLIE BRICUSSE

Music by
JOHN WILLIAMS

Theme from

CAROLINE IN THE CITY

By
JONATHAN WOLFF

Theme from
"CHICAGO HOPE"

Music by
MARK ISHAM

"Chicago Hope" - 2 - 1

COLORS OF THE WIND

Lyrics by
STEPHEN SCHWARTZ

Music by
ALAN MENKEN

CORNER OF THE SKY

Words and Music by
STEPHEN SCHWARTZ

Ev-'ry-thing has its sea - son,
Ev-'ry man has his day - dreams,
may-be some mist - y day,__ you'll

Corner of the Sky - 5 - 1

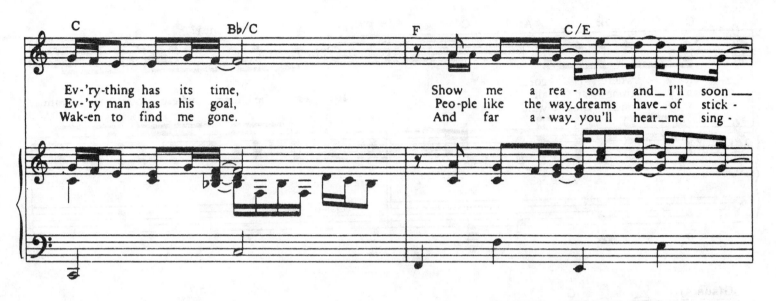

of the sky. ___

DAY BY DAY

Words and Music by
STEPHEN SCHWARTZ

Day by Day - 3 - 1

DAYS OF WINE AND ROSES

Words by
JOHNNY MERCER

Music by
HENRY MANCINI

Days of Wine and Roses - 2 - 1

Theme from

DR. QUINN MEDICINE WOMAN

By
WILLIAM OLVIS

Dr. Quinn Medicine Woman - 2 - 1

DREAMING OF YOU

Moderately ♩ = 88

Words and Music by
TOM SNOW and
FRANNE GOLDE

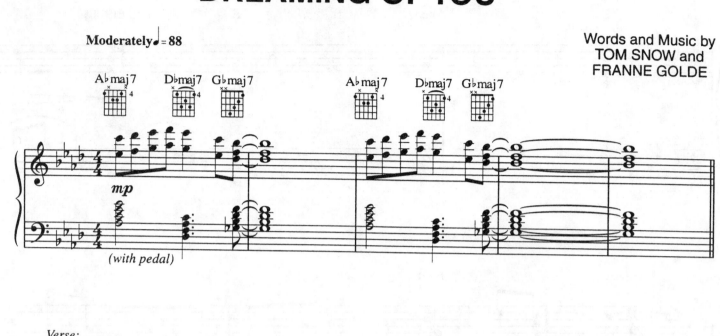

(with pedal)

Verse:

1. Late at night when all the world___ is sleep-ing, I stay up and think of you.___ And I

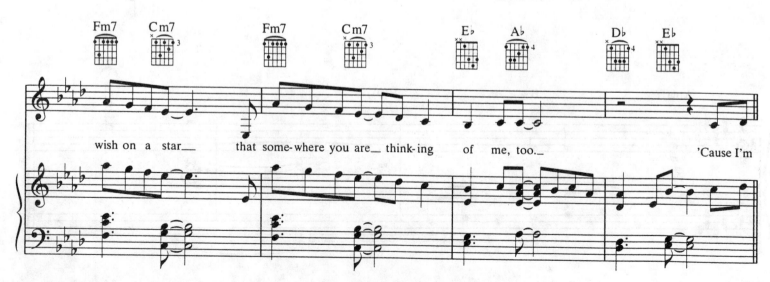

wish on a star___ that some-where you are___ think-ing of me, too.___ 'Cause I'm

Chorus:

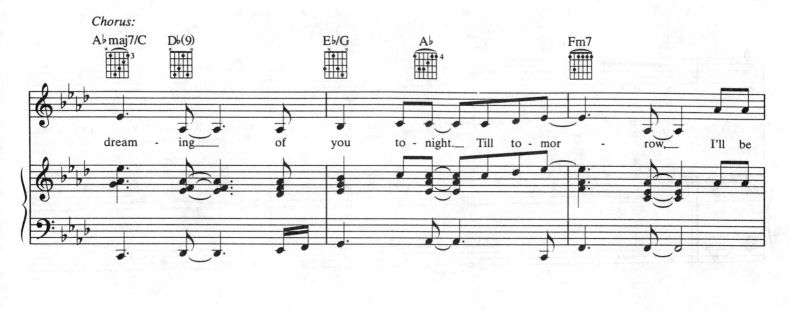

dream - ing___ of you to - night.___ Till to - mor - row,___ I'll be

hold - ing you tight.___ And there's no - where in___ the world I'd rath - er be than

here in my room,___ dream - ing a - bout___ you and me.___

ER
(Main Theme)

Composed by
JAMES NEWTON HOWARD

ER - 2 - 1

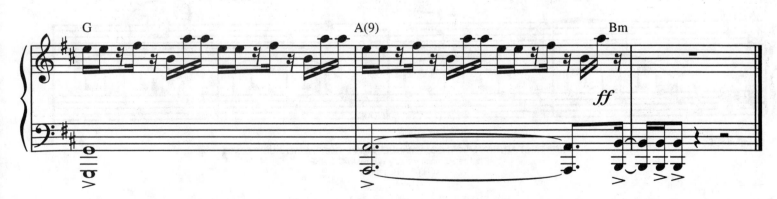

ER - 2 - 2

From "A STAR IS BORN"

EVERGREEN

Words by
PAUL WILLIAMS

Music by
BARBRA STREISAND

Evergreen - 6 - 1

FOR THE FIRST TIME

Words and Music by
JAMES NEWTON HOWARD,
ALLAN RICH and JUD FRIEDMAN

Slowly ♩ = 62

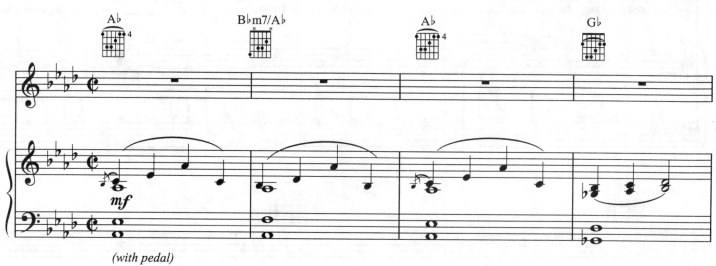

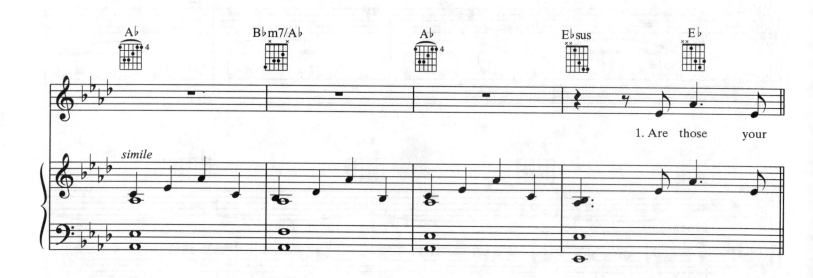

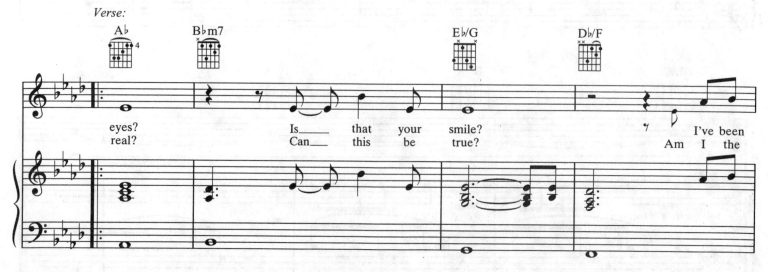

For the First Time - 6 - 1

FOR YOU I WILL

Words and Music by
DIANE WARREN

For You I Will - 5 - 1

FRIENDS AND LOVERS
(Both to Each Other)

Words and Music by
PAUL GORDON and JAY GRUSKA

Medium Ballad

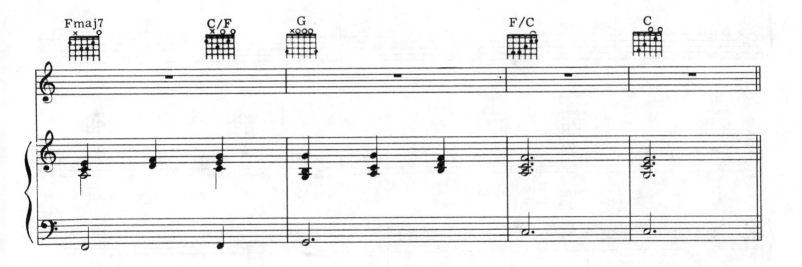

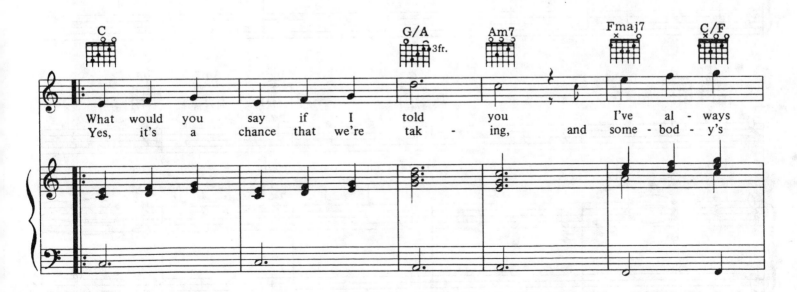

What would you say if I told you, I've al-ways
Yes, it's a chance that we're tak- ing, and some-bod- y's

Friends and Lovers - 4 - 1

want - ed   to   hold ____   you.   I   don't   know   what   we're   a - fraid
heart   may   be   break ____   ing.   But   we   can't   stop   what's   in - side

of;   noth - ing   would   change   if   we   made   love.   }   'Cause I'll
us,   our   love   for   each   oth - er   will   guide   us.

be   your   friend,   and I'll   be   your

lov - er.   Well, I   know   in   our   hearts   we   a - gree ____

HEART

Words and Music by
RICHARD ADLER and
JERRY ROSS

HE LOVES AND SHE LOVES

Music and Lyrics by
GEORGE GERSHWIN
and IRA GERSHWIN

He Loves and She Loves - 4 - 1

From the Original Motion Picture Soundtrack "DON JUAN DeMARCO"
HAVE YOU EVER REALLY LOVED A WOMAN?

Lyrics by
BRYAN ADAMS and
ROBERT JOHN "MUTT" LANGE

Music by
MICHAEL KAMEN

Chorus:

love_____ a wom-an._____ When

you love a wom-an, you tell her that she's real-ly want-ed. When

you love a wom-an, you tell her that she's_____ the one.___

She needs some-bod-y to tell her that it's gon-na last_____ for-ev-er. So

HEY, LOOK ME OVER

Music by
CY COLEMAN

Lyrics by
CAROLYN LEIGH

Hey, Look Me Over - 3 - 1

Interlude (ad lib.)

No-bod-y in the world was ev-er with-out a pray'r;

How can you win the world, if no-bod-y knows you're there.

Kid, when you need the crowd, the tick-ets are hard to sell;

Still you can lead the crowd, if you can get up and yell:

D.S. %

HOME

Words and Music by
CHARLIE SMALLS

things I've been know-ing. Wind that makes the tall trees bend in - to lean-ing,
love and af - fec - tion. And just may-be I can con-vince time to slow up,

sud - den - ly the snow - flakes that fall have a mean - ing, sprink - ling_____ the
giv - ing me e - nough time in my life to grow up. Time be my

scene makes it_____ all clean.
friend, let me start a - gain.

Sud-den-ly my world's gone and changed its face but I still know where I'm

go - ing. I have had my mind spun a - round in space and yet I've

watched it grow - ing. If you're lis - 'ning God, please don't

make it hard to know if we should be-lieve the things that we see. Tell us

should we run a-way, should we try and stay or would it be bet-ter just to let things be?

Liv-ing here in this brand new world might be a fan-ta-sy but it taught me to love so it's real to me. And I've

learned that we must look in-side our hearts to find a world full of love like yours and mine, like home.

From the Touchstone Motion Picture "CON AIR"

HOW DO I LIVE

Words and Music by
DIANE WARREN

How Do I Live - 4 - 1

Repeat ad lib. and fade
(vocal 1st time only)

Verse 2:
Without you, there'd be no sun in my sky,
There would be no love in my life,
There'd be no world left for me.
And I, baby, I don't know what I would do,
I'd be lost if I lost you.
If you ever leave,
Baby, you would take away everything real in my life.
And tell me now...
(To Chorus:)

From the Warner Bros. Motion Picture "BEST FRIENDS"

HOW DO YOU KEEP THE MUSIC PLAYING?

Words by
ALAN and MARILYN BERGMAN

Music by
MICHEL LEGRAND

How Do You Keep the Music Playing? - 4 - 1

I BELIEVE I CAN FLY

Words and Music by
R. KELLY

From the Original Soundtrack Album "THE PREACHER'S WIFE"

I BELIEVE IN YOU AND ME

Words and Music by
SANDY LINZER and DAVID WOLFERT

I Believe in You and Me - 4 - 1

128

I Believe in You and Me - 4 - 2

Verse 2:
I will never leave your side,
I will never hurt your pride.
When all the chips are down,
I will always be around,
Just to be right where you are, my love.
Oh, I love you, boy.
I will never leave you out,
I will always let you in
To places no one has ever been.
Deep inside, can't you see?
I believe in you and me.
(To Bridge:)

I CROSS MY HEART

Words and Music by
STEVE DORFF and ERIC KAZ

I Cross My Heart - 5 - 1

Additional Lyrics

2. You will always be the miracle
   That makes my life complete.
   And as long as there's a breath in me
   I'll make yours just as sweet.
   As we look into the future,
   It's as far as we can see.
   So let's make each tomorrow
   Be the best that it can be.
   (To Chorus)

From the Motion Picture "ROBIN HOOD: PRINCE OF THIEVES"

(EVERYTHING I DO) I DO IT FOR YOU

Written by
BRYAN ADAMS, ROBERT JOHN LANGE
and MICHAEL KAMEN

Look in-to my eyes,— you will see—
Look in-to your heart,— you will find— there's

what you mean to— me.
noth - ing there to— hide.

Search your heart,— search your
So, take me as I am, take my

(Everything I Do) I Do It for You - 4 - 1

From Touchstone Pictures' "ARMAGEDDON"

I DON'T WANT TO MISS A THING

Words and Music by
DIANE WARREN

Chorus:

miss you, ba - by, and I don't wan - na miss a thing.___ 'Coz e - ven when I dream of you,___

the sweet - est dream would nev - er do.___ I'd still miss you, ba - by, and I don't wan - na miss a thing._

Repeat ad lib. and fade

From the Motion Picture "THE MIRROR HAS TWO FACES"

I FINALLY FOUND SOMEONE

Words and Music by
BARBRA STREISAND, MARVIN HAMLISCH,
R. J. LANGE and BRYAN ADAMS

I Finally Found Someone - 8 - 1

It's bet-ter than it's ev - er been_ 'cause we can talk it { through.
{ through,_ yeah._

My fa - v'rite line_____ was, "Can I call you some - time?"_

It's all you had to say_ to take my breath a - way._

Chorus:

This is it! Oh,_____ I fi - n'lly

150

153

I Finally Found Someone - 8 - 7

From the Motion Picture "THE BODYGUARD"

I WILL ALWAYS LOVE YOU

Words and Music by
DOLLY PARTON

I Will Always Love You - 3 - 1

157

I WILL REMEMBER YOU

Words and Music by
SARAH McLACHLAN, SEAMUS EGAN
and DAVE MERENDA

Verse 2:
So afraid to love you,
More afraid to lose.
I'm clinging to a past
That doesn't let me choose.
Where once there was a darkness,
A deep and endless night,
You gave me everything you had,
Oh, you gave me life.
(To Chorus:)

(Optional Verse 1 — Album version)
Remember the good times that we had,
I let them slip away from us when things got bad.
Now clearly I first saw you smiling in the sun.
I wanna feel your warmth upon me,
I wanna be the one.
(To Chorus:)

From the Columbia Motion Picture "ICE CASTLES"

THEME FROM ICE CASTLES
(Through the Eyes of Love)

Lyrics by CAROLE BAYER SAGER
Music by MARVIN HAMLISCH

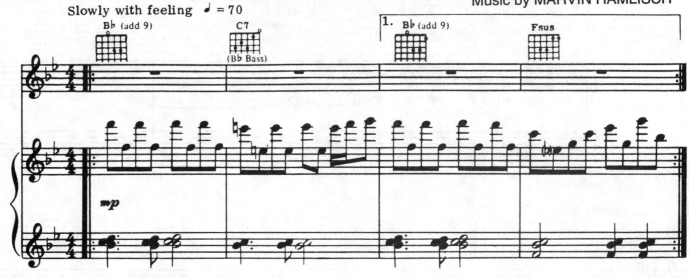

1. Please,   don't let this feel - ing
2. now   I can take the
3. Please,   don't let this feel - ing

(cross hands)

end. It's ev-'ry-thing I am, ev-'ry-thing I want to be.
time.   I can see my life as it comes up shin - ing now.
end. It might not come a - gain and I want to re - mem - ber

Theme From Ice Castles - 3 - 1

now I do be-lieve that e-ven in the storm we'll find _____ some

light. Know-ing you're be-side me I'm all_ right. _____

D.S. al Coda

Coda

through the eyes _____ of love.

IF MY FRIENDS COULD SEE ME NOW!

Music by
CY COLEMAN

Lyric by
DOROTHY FIELDS

If My Friends Could See Me Now! - 3 - 1

Theme from "FRIENDS"

I'LL BE THERE FOR YOU

Words by
DAVID CRANE, MARTA KAUFFMAN, ALLEE WILLIS,
PHIL SOLEM and DANNY WILDE

Music by
MICHAEL SKLOFF

* Guitar fill reads 8va.

I'll Be There for You - 6 - 3

I'LL NEVER FALL IN LOVE AGAIN

Words by
HAL DAVID

Music by
BURT BACHARACH

Theme from the Motion Picture "WITH HONORS"

I'LL REMEMBER

Words and Music by
PATRICK LEONARD,
MADONNA CICCONE and RICHARD PAGE

I'll Remember - 4 - 1

180

I'll remember. ___ Mm. ___ I learned ___

to let go ___ of the il-lu-sion that we can pos-ses. I learned ___

to let go. ___ I tra-vel in still-ness. And I'll re-mem-ber ___

Lyrics:
hap-pi-ness. I'll re-mem-ber. Mm.

D.S. 𝄋 (2nd lyric) al Coda ⊕

i'll re-mem-ber. Mm. And I'll re-

Coda ⊕

Repeat and fade

I'll re-mem-ber.

Though I've nev-er been a-fraid to cry, now I fin-al-ly have a rea-son why. I'll re-mem-ber.

I'VE GOTTA BE ME

Music and Lyrics by
WALTER MARKS

I've Gotta Be Me - 3 - 2

THE JETSONS MAIN THEME
from "THE JETSONS"

Words and Music by WILLIAM HANNA,
JOSEPH BARBERA and HOYT CURTIN

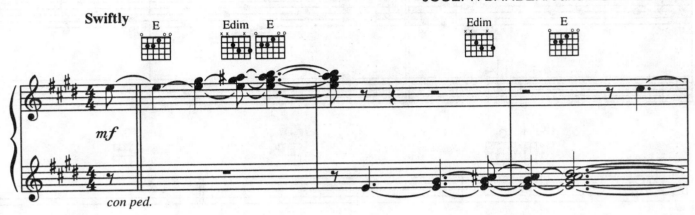

Meet George Jet - son!

Jetsons Main Theme - 3 - 1

From the Twentieth Century Fox Motion Picture "ANASTASIA"

JOURNEY TO THE PAST

Lyrics by
LYNN AHRENS

Music by
STEPHEN FLAHERTY

Journey to the Past - 8 - 1

189

Journey to the Past - 8 - 2

From the Twentieth Century Fox Television Series

KING OF THE HILL

Words and Music by
ROGER CLYNE, BRIAN BLUSH,
ARTHUR EDWARDS and PAUL NAFFAH

King of the Hill - 2 - 1

KISS FROM A ROSE

Words and Music by
SEAL

Bridge:

I've been kissed by a rose___ on the grey.___ I've been
I've _____ been

kissed by a rose.___ I've been kissed by a rose___ on the grey.
kissed by a rose___ on the grey. I've ___

_____ I've been kissed by a rose___
I've _____ been kissed by a rose___ on the grey.___

Verse 3:

There is so much a man can

KISSING YOU
(Love Theme From "ROMEO + JULIET")

Words and Music by
DES'REE and TIM ATACK

Theme from the TV Series "L.A. LAW"

L.A. LAW
(Main Title)

By
MIKE POST

L.A. Law - 3 - 1

Hair

LET THE SUNSHINE IN

Words by
JAMES RADO
and GEROME RAGNI

Music by
GALT MacDERMOT

LINUS AND LUCY

By VINCE GUARALDI

Linus and Lucy - 2 - 1

From Warner Bros. "QUEST FOR CAMELOT"

LOOKING THROUGH YOUR EYES

Words and Music by
CAROLE BAYER SAGER
and DAVID FOSTER

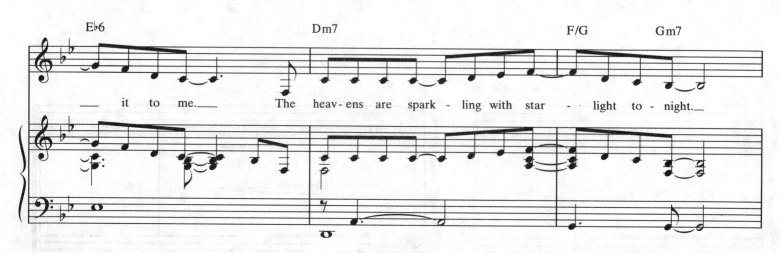

Looking Through Your Eyes - 5 - 1

Looking Through Your Eyes-5-5

Theme from the TV Series "MARRIED . . . WITH CHILDREN"

LOVE AND MARRIAGE

Words by
SAMMY CAHN

Music by
JAMES VAN HEUSEN

LOVE AND MAR - RIAGE, LOVE AND MAR - RIAGE,

Go to-geth - er like a horse and car - riage, This I tell ya
It's an in - sti - tute you can't dis - par - age, ask the lo - cal

Love and Marriage - 3 - 1

223

Love and Marriage - 3 - 3

From the Broadway Musical "42ND STREET"

LULLABY OF BROADWAY

Words by
AL DUBIN

Music by
HARRY WARREN

Lullaby of Broadway - 3 - 1

Theme from the PBS Series "MASTERPIECE THEATRE"

THE MASTERPIECE

By J.J. MOURET
and PAUL PARNES

Majestically

The Masterpiece - 3 - 1

To Coda II

To Coda I

mf

From the WARNER BROS. TV Show "THE DREW CAREY SHOW"

MOON OVER PARMA

Words and Music by
ROBERT F. McGUIRE

Moon over Parma - 3 - 2

Moon Over Parma - 3 - 3

MY FRIEND

Music by
CY COLEMAN

Lyrics by
IRA GASMAN

My Friend - 5 - 1

MY OWN TRUE LOVE
(Tara Theme)

Words by
MACK DAVID

Music by
MAX STEINER

My Own True Love - 2 - 1

col 8

Theme from the PBS Television Series "MYSTERY"

MYSTERY

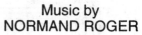

Music by
NORMAND ROGER

Mystery - 3 - 1

242

From the Broadway Musical "MERRILY WE ROLL ALONG"

NOT A DAY GOES BY

Music and Lyrics by
STEPHEN SONDHEIM

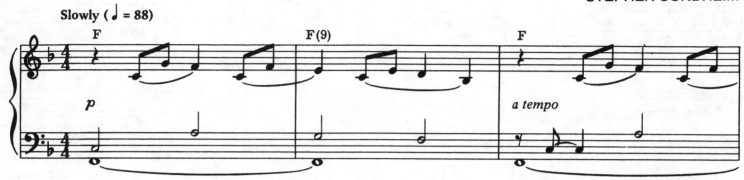

Not A Day Goes By,_____ not a sin-gle day
Not A Day Goes By,_____ not a sin-gle day

you're not some-where a part of my life_____ and I need you to stay
but you're some-where a part of my life_____ and it looks like you'll stay

Not a Day Goes By - 4 - 1

From the Broadway Musical "SWEENEY TODD"

NOT WHILE I'M AROUND

Music and Lyrics by
STEPHEN SONDHEIM

Allegretto (♩ = 176)

Not to wor-ry, Not to wor-ry, I may not be smart, but I ain't

dumb. Let me do it, Put me to it, Show me some-thing I can o-ver-

come. Not to wor-ry, chum.

Andante placido (♩ = 112)

Poco rubato

Noth-ing's gon-na harm you, Not while I'm a-round. ___

Not While I'm Around - 3 - 1

Noth-ing's gon - na harm you, no sir, Not while I'm a - round. ___

De - mons are prowl - ing ev - 'ry - where, Now - a - days. ___

I'll send 'em howl - ing, I don't care, I got ways. ___

No-one's gon-na hurt you, No-one's gon-na dare. __

From the TV Series "NYPD BLUE"

THEME FROM "NYPD BLUE"

Music by
MIKE POST

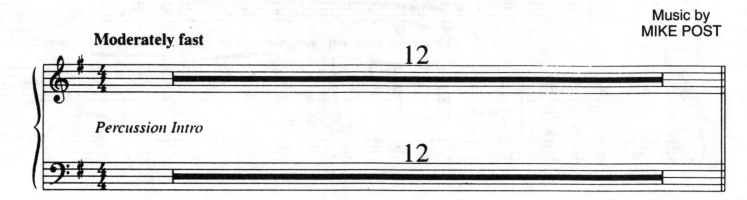

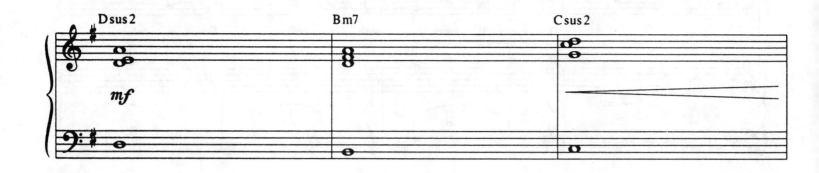

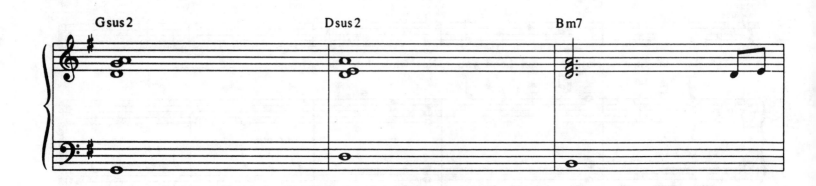

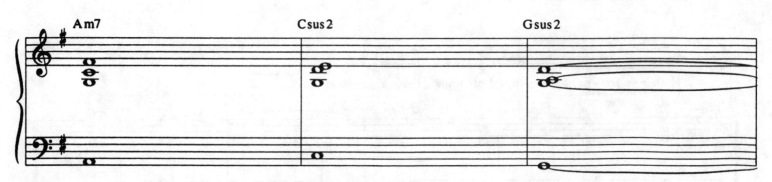

Theme from "NYPD Blue" - 2 - 1

Theme from "NYPD Blue" - 2 - 2

Recorded by FRANK SINATRA on REPRISE Records
From the United Artists Motion Picture "NEW YORK, NEW YORK"

THEME FROM NEW YORK, NEW YORK

Words by
FRED EBB

Music by
JOHN KANDER

Theme From New York, New York - 5 - 1

York. If I can make it there, ___ I'd make it

an - y - where, ___ It's up to you, New York, New

York.

D. S. al Coda

Coda

king of the hill, head of the list, cream of the crop at the top of the heap.

ON A CLEAR DAY
(You Can See Forever)

Lyrics by
ALAN JAY LERNER

Music by
BURTON LANE

On a clear day___ Rise and look a-round you___

And you'll see who___ you are.

On a clear day___ How it will as-tound you___

On a Clear Day - 3 - 1

From the M-G-M Motion Picture "THE HARVEY GIRLS"

ON THE ATCHISON, TOPEKA AND THE SANTA FE

Lyric by
JOHNNY MERCER

Music by
HARRY WARREN

On the Atchison, Topeka and the Santa Fe - 2 - 1

On the Atchison, Topeka and the Santa Fe - 2 - 2

Theme Song from the Mirisch-G&E Production, "THE PINK PANTHER," a United Artists Release

THE PINK PANTHER

Music by
HENRY MANCINI

Moderately Mysterioso

The Pink Panther - 2 - 1

The Pink Panther - 2 - 2

PUT ON A HAPPY FACE

Lyrics by
LEE ADAMS

Music by
CHARLES STROUSE

Put on a Happy Face - 2 - 1

From the Motion Picture "THE WIZARD OF OZ"

OVER THE RAINBOW

Lyric by
E.Y. HARBURG

Music by
HAROLD ARLEN

From the Twentieth Century Fox Motion Picture "ANASTASIA"

ONCE UPON A DECEMBER

Lyrics by
LYNN AHRENS

Music by
STEPHEN FLAHERTY

RAGTIME

Lyrics by
LYNN AHRENS

Music by
STEPHEN FLAHERTY

Ragtime - 6 - 1

giv - ing the na - tion a   new syn - co - pa - tion. The   peo - ple called it Rag - time!

(Cakewalk)

And there was dis - tant mu - sic, skip-ping a beat, sing-ing a dream. La - la-la-la-

la! A strange, in - sis - tant mu - sic, put-ting out heat, pick-ing up steam. La - la-la-la-

la! The sound of dis - tant thun - der sud - den - ly start - ing to

From the 20th Century-Fox Film "BUTCH CASSIDY AND THE SUNDANCE KID"

RAINDROPS KEEP FALLING ON MY HEAD

Words by
HAL DAVID

Music by
BURT BACHARACH

Raindrops Keep Falling on My Head - 4 - 1

soon be turn - in' red. Cry - in's not for me cause

I'm nev - er gon - na stop the rain by com-plain-in'. Be - cause I'm

free noth - in's wor - ry - in' me. _____

From the Twentieth Century-Fox Motion Picture "THE ROSE"

THE ROSE

Words and Music by
AMANDA McBROOM

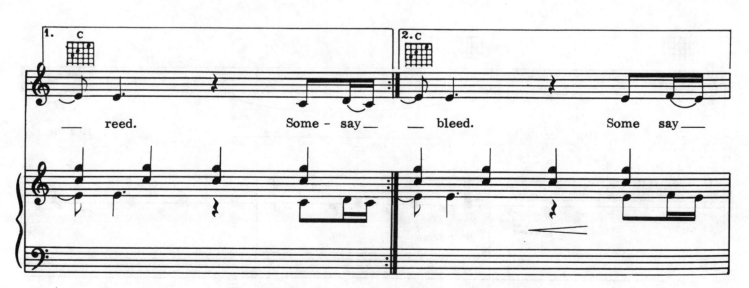

The Rose - 4 - 1

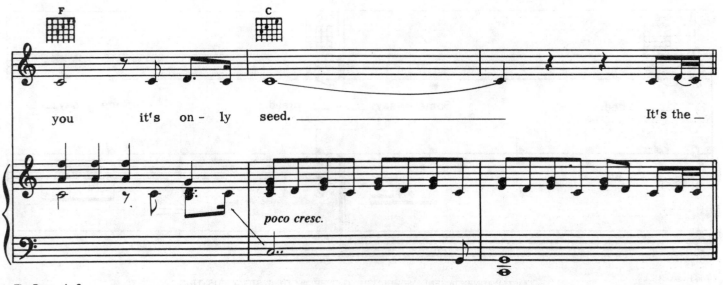

love _____ it is a hun - ger _____ an end - less ach - ing

need. _____ I say _ love it is a flow - er _____ and

poco rit. - - - - - - - *a tempo*

you it's on - ly seed. _____ It's the _

poco cresc.

From the Twentieth Century Fox Television Series
Ally McBeal

SEARCHIN' MY SOUL

Words and Music by
VONDA SHEPARD and
HOWARD GORDON

Chorus:

I've de-cid-ed to move on. Gon-na leave____ all my wor-

ries____ be-hind.____

D.S. 𝄋 *al Coda*

Coda

From the Broadway Musical "LITTLE ME"

REAL LIVE GIRL

Music by
CY COLEMAN

Lyrics by
CAROLYN LEIGH

Old-fashioned waltz tempo *(moderately bright)*

Refrain

Par - don me, miss, but I've nev - er done this with a REAL LIVE
Noth - ing can beat get - ting swept off your feet by a REAL LIVE

GIRL, _____ Strayed off the farm with an ac - tu - al arm - ful of
GIRL, _____ Dreams in your bunk don't com - pare with a hunk of a

REAL LIVE GIRL. _____ Par - don me if your af - fec -
REAL LIVE GIRL. _____ Speak - ing of mir - a - cles,

fec - tion - ate squeeze. Fogs up my gog - gles and buck - les my knees,
this must be it, Just when I start - ed to learn how to knit,

*From the Motion Picture "M*A*S*H"*

SONG FROM M*A*S*H

Words and Music by
MIKE ALTMAN and JOHNNY MANDEL

Song From M*A*S*H - 2 - 1

1. Try to find a way to make
   All our little joys relate
   Without that ever-present hate
   But now I know that it's too late.
   And, Chorus

3. The game of life is hard to play,
   I'm going to lose it anyway,
   The losing card I'll someday lay,
   So this is all I have to say.
   That: Chorus

4. The only way to win, is cheat
   And lay it down before I'm beat,
   And to another give a seat
   For that's the only painless feat.
   'Cause: Chorus

5. The sword of time will pierce our skins,
   It doesn't hurt when it begins
   But as it works it's way on in,
   The pain grows stronger, watch it grin.
   For: Chorus

6. A brave man once requested me
   To answer questions that are key,
   Is it to be or not to be
   And I replied; "Oh, why ask me."
   'Cause: Chorus

SEND IN THE CLOWNS
(From "A Little Night Music")

Music and Lyrics by
STEPHEN SONDHEIM

This arrangement includes Mr. Sondheim's revised lyrics for Barbra Streisand's recording.

Send in the Clowns - 3 - 1

From the PBS TV Show "SESAME STREET"

SING

Words and Music by
JOE RAPOSO

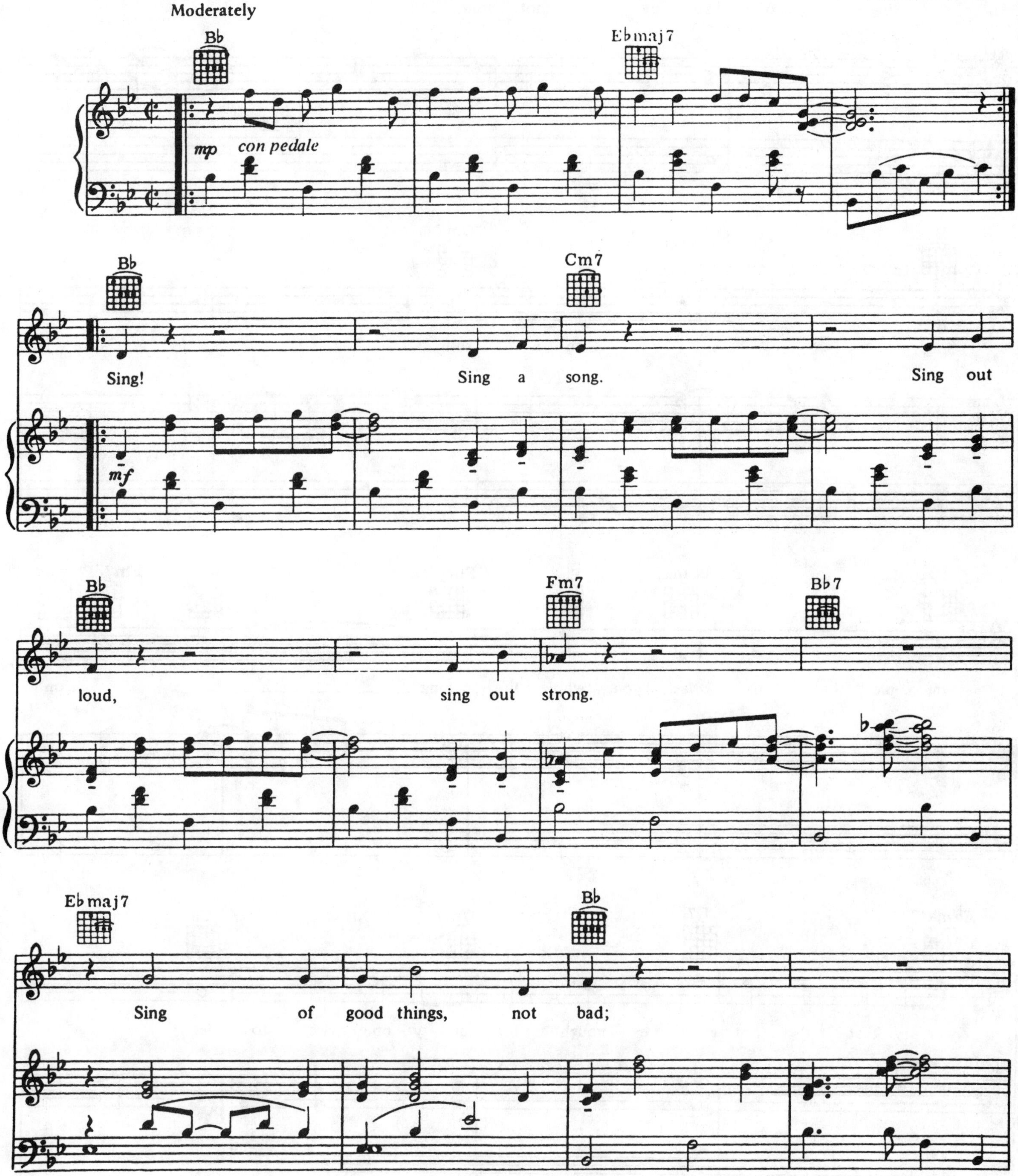

Sing! Sing a song. Sing out

loud, sing out strong.

Sing of good things, not bad;

Sing - 3 - 1

THEME FROM "THE SIMPSONS"

Music by
DANNY ELFMAN

Theme From "The Simpsons" - 4 - 2

308

SOMETHING'S GOTTA GIVE

Words and Music by
JOHNNY MERCER

When an ir - re - sist - i - ble force such as you meets an old im - mov - a - ble ob - ject like me, You can bet as sure as you live, SOME-THING'S GOT-TA GIVE, SOME-THING'S

Something's Gotta Give - 4 - 1

312

Something's Gotta Give - 4 - 3

From the Motion Pictures "STAR WARS" and "THE EMPIRE STRIKES BACK"
A Lucasfilm Ltd. Production - A Twentieth Century-Fox Release

STAR WARS
(Main Theme)

Music by JOHN WILLIAMS

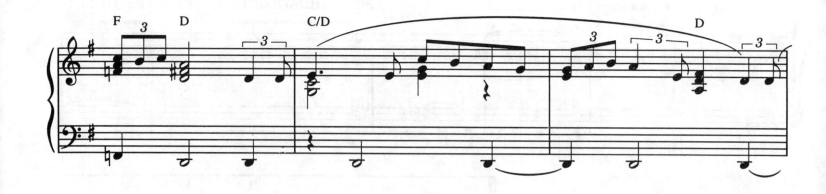

Star Wars (Main Theme) - 2 - 1

Star Wars (Maim Theme) - 2 - 2

THE SUMMER KNOWS
(Theme from "SUMMER OF 42")

Lyrics by
ALAN and MARILYN BERGMAN

Music by
MICHEL LEGRAND

The Summer Knows - 2 - 1

SUMMERTIME

From *Porgy and Bess* ®
By GEORGE GERSHWIN,
DU BOSE and DOROTHY HEYWARD
and IRA GERSHWIN

Summertime - 4 - 1

320

Summertime - 4 - 3

SUNRISE, SUNSET

Lyrics by
SHELDON HARNICK

Music by
JERRY BOCK

Sunrise, Sunset - 4 - 1

Chorus

STREETS OF PHILADELPHIA

Words and Music by
BRUCE SPRINGSTEEN

Moderately, with a beat ♩ = 96

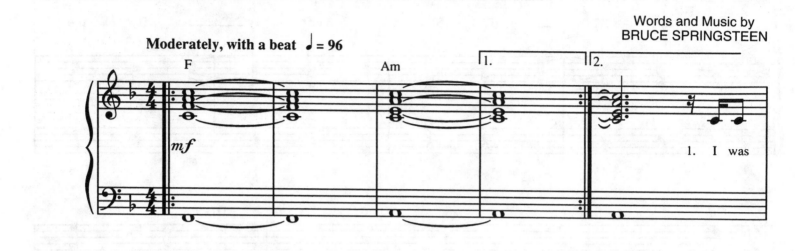

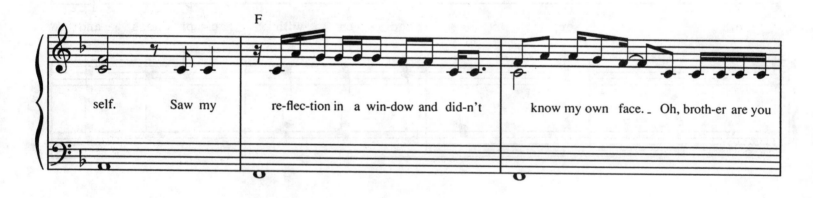

Streets of Philadelphia - 3 - 1

And my clothes don't fit me no more; — I walked a thou-sand miles — just to —

D.S. 𝄋 al Coda

—slip this skin. —

⊕ Coda

la — la la la la. —

1.2. La — la la la la
3.4.(etc.) *Instrumental repeat & fade*

Repeat ad lib. and fade

la — la la la la la — la la la la la — la la la la. —

Verse 2:
I walked the avenue till my legs felt like stone.
I heard the voices of friends vanished and gone.
At night I could hear the blood in my veins
Just as black and whispering as the rain
On the streets of Philadelphia.
(To Chorus:)

Verse 3:
The night has fallen. I'm lyin' awake.
I can feel myself fading away.
So, receive me, brother, with your faithless kiss,
Or will we leave each other alone like this
On the streets of Philadelphia?
(To Chorus:)

THAT'S WHAT FRIENDS ARE FOR

Words and Music by
CAROLE BAYER SAGER and BURT BACHARACH

That's What Friends Are For - 3 - 1

For good - times, and bad_ times
in good - times, in bad_ times
I'll be on_ your side for - ev - er

more.
That's what friends_ are for

for.

D.S. al Coda

Coda

for.

Repeat and fade
Vocal ad lib.

From the Twentieth Century Fox Motion Picture

THAT THING YOU DO!

Words and Music by
ADAM SCHLESINGER

From the Warner Bros. TV Movie "THE THORN BIRDS"

THE THORN BIRDS THEME

Music by
HENRY MANCINI

The Thorn Birds Theme - 2 - 1

Theme from "THE BUGS BUNNY SHOW"

THIS IS IT!

Words and Music by
MACK DAVID and JERRY LIVINGSTON

This Is It! - 3 - 1

TO LIFE

Lyrics by
SHELDON HARNICK

Music by
JERRY BOCK

To Life - 4 - 1

344

To Life - 4 - 4

From the Motion Picture "ANNIE"

TOMORROW

Lyric by
MARTIN CHARNIN

Music by
CHARLES STROUSE

Tomorrow - 3 - 1

From *"CITY of ANGELS"*

THE UNFEELING KISS

By
GABRIEL YARED

Moderately fast ($\quad\!\! = 80$)
"Central Market"

mp

(with pedal)

The Unfeeling Kiss - 6 - 1

Slowly (♩ = 80)

"An Angel Falls"

Slower (♩ = 70)

"The Unfeeling Kiss"

pp

sub. p

dim.

Paramount Pictures Presents A Lorimar-Martin Elfand Production-A Taylor Hackford Film
"AN OFFICER AND A GENTLEMAN"

UP WHERE WE BELONG

Words by
WILL JENNINGS

Music by
BUFFY SAINTE-MARIE and JACK NITZSCHE

Verse 2:
Some hang on to "used-to-be",
Live their lives looking behind.
All we have is here and now;
All our life, out there to find.
The road is long.
There are mountains in our way,
But we climb them a step every day.

WALK WITH YOU
(Theme from "Touched By An Angel")

Music and Lyrics by
MARC LICHTMAN

WHEELS OF A DREAM

Lyrics by
LYNN AHRENS

Music by
STEPHEN FLAHERTY

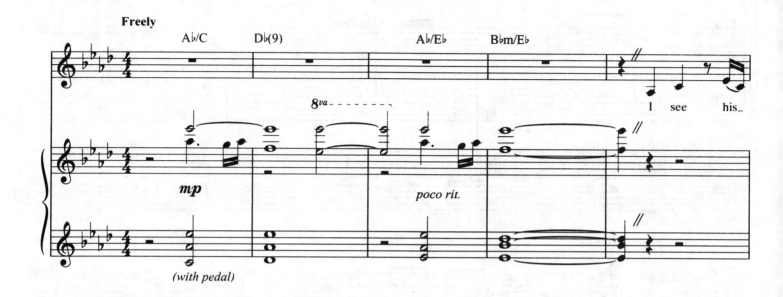

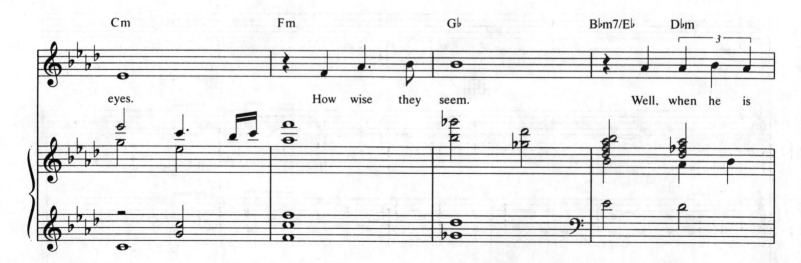

Wheels of a Dream - 10 - 1

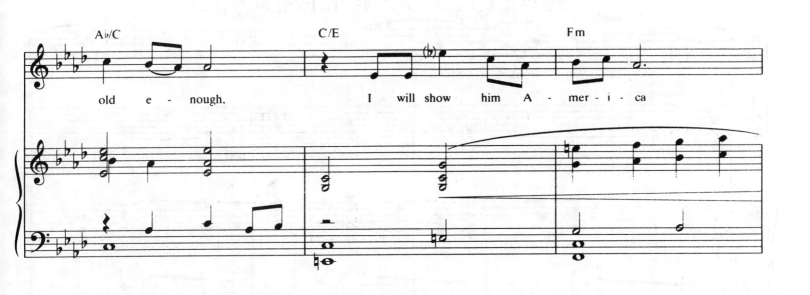

old e - nough.　I will show him A - mer - i - ca

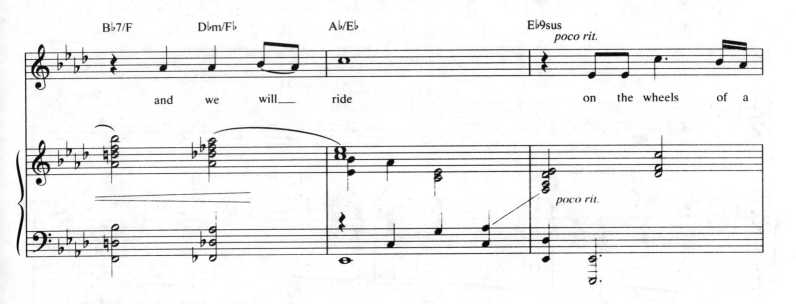

and　we will___ ride　on the wheels of a

dream..._____ We'll go down_

Coalhouse:

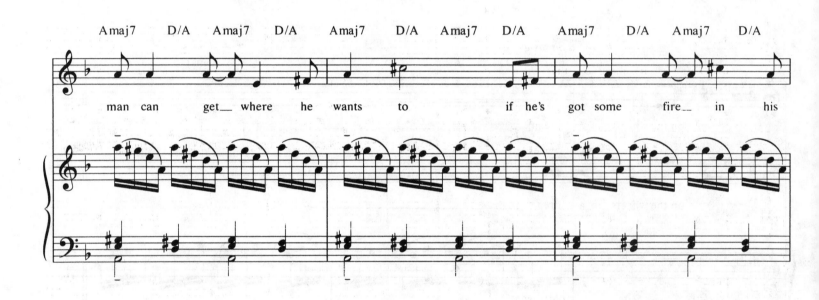

E♭m E♭m/D♭ Cm7(♯5)

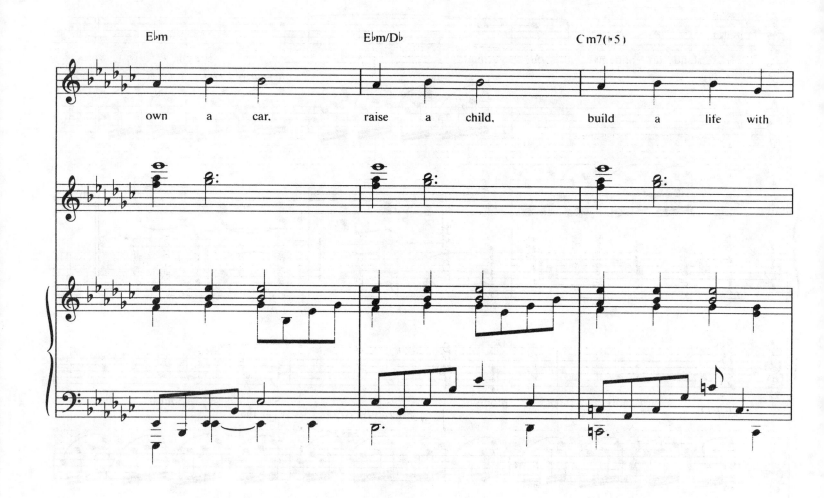

own a car. raise a child. build a life with

poco rall.

you..._____ with

poco rall.

WHEN I LOOK AT YOU

**Lyrics by
NAN KNIGHTON**

**Music by
FRANK WILDHORN**

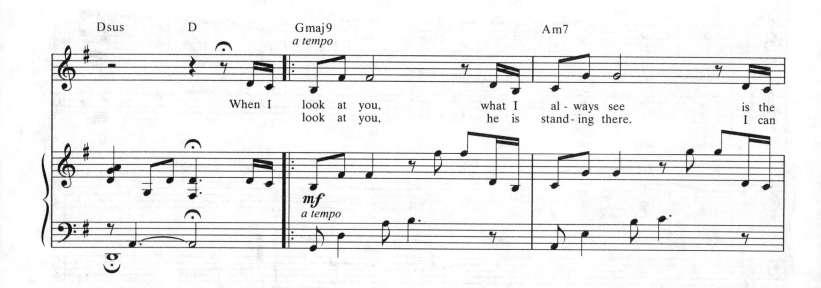

When I Look at You - 5 - 1

A WHOLE NEW WORLD

Words by
TIM RICE

Music by
ALAN MENKEN

Moderately slow, and sweetly

From the Original Motion Picture Soundtrack "BEACHES"

THE WIND BENEATH MY WINGS

**Words and Music by
LARRY HENLEY and JEFF SILBAR**

The Wind Beneath My Wings - 7 - 4

389

The Wind Beneath My Wings - 7 - 6

Theme from the TV Series "THE X-FILES"

THEME FROM "THE X-FILES"

Music by
MARK SNOW

Moderately ♩ = 96

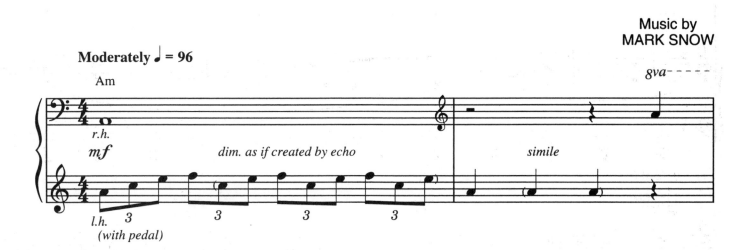

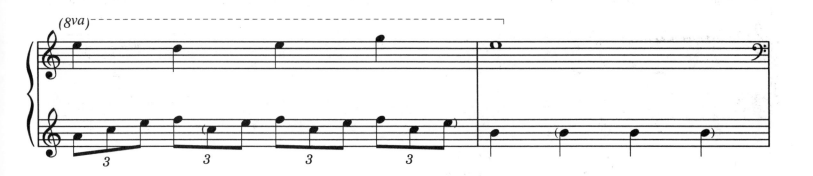

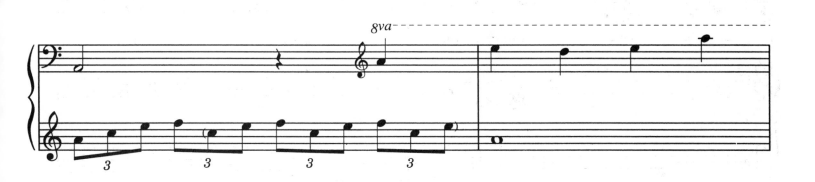

Theme from The X-Files - 6 - 1

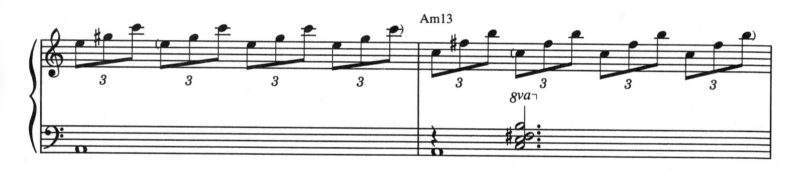

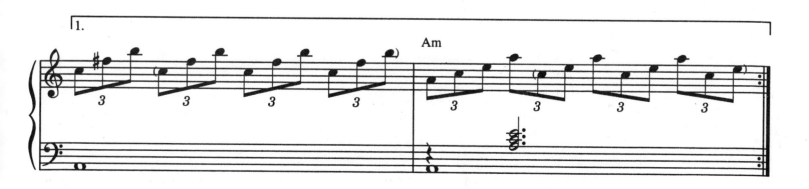

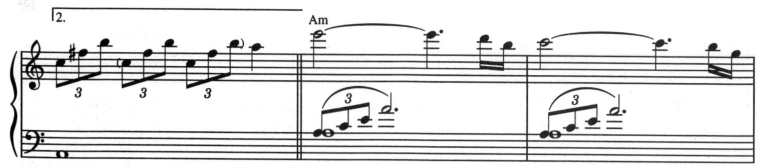

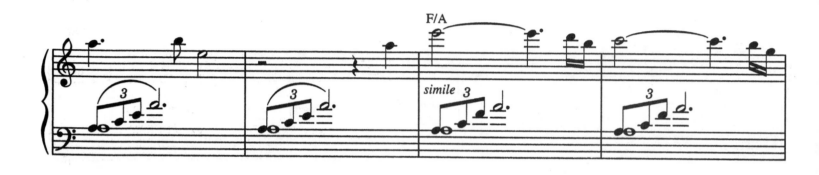

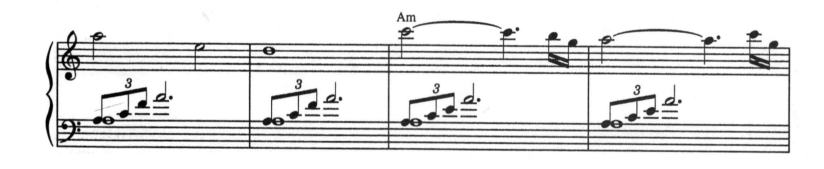

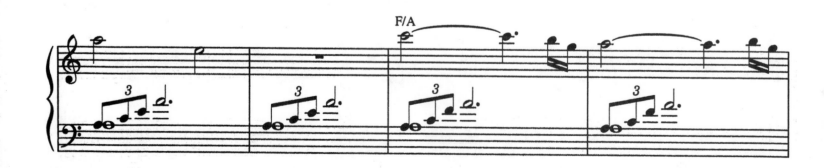

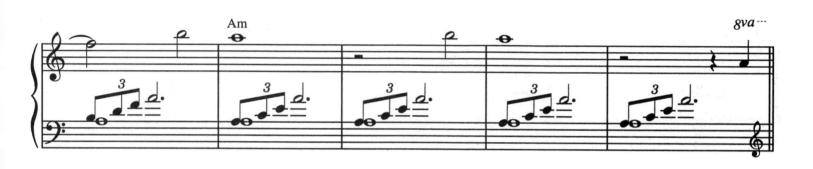

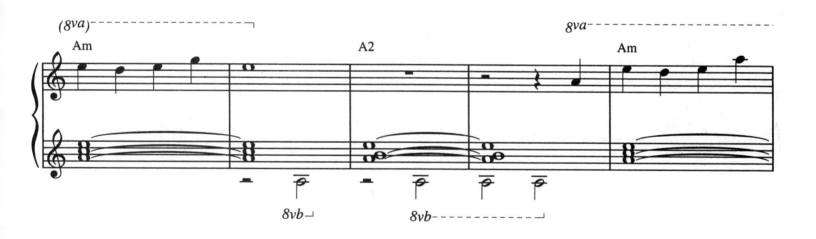

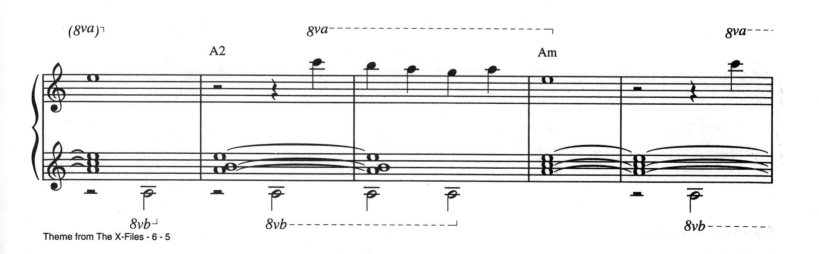

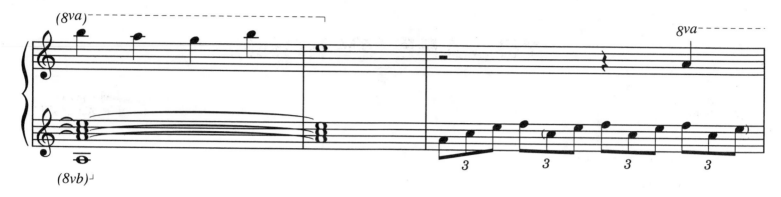

YOU ARE MY HOME

Lyrics by
NAN KNIGHTON

Music by
FRANK WILDHORN